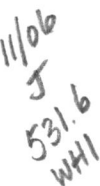

Energy Everywhere

Patty Whitehouse

Rourke
Publishing LLC
Vero Beach, Florida 32964

© 2007 Rourke Publishing LLC

All rights reserved. No part of this book may be reproduced or utilized in any form or by any means, electronic or mechanical including photocopying, recording, or by any information storage and retrieval system without permission in writing from the publisher.

www.rourkepublishing.com

PHOTO CREDITS: © constructionphotographs.com: pages 6, 7, 10, 14, 16, 17; © David and Patricia Armentrout: pages 4, 5, 8, 9, 13, 18, 22; © PIR: pages 11, 15, 20, 21; © Tomaz Levstek: page 19; © Daniel Hyams: page 12

Editor: Robert Stengard-Olliges

Cover and interior design by Nicola Stratford

Library of Congress Cataloging-in-Publication Data

Whitehouse, Patricia, 1958-
 Energy everywhere / Patty Whitehouse.
     p. cm. -- (Construction forces)
 Includes index.
 ISBN 1-60044-189-0 (hardcover)
 ISBN 1-59515-553-8 (softcover)
  1. Power resources--Juvenile literature. 2. Energy consumption--Juvenile literature. 3. Building sites--Juvenile literature. I. Title. II. Series: Whitehouse, Patricia, 1958- Construction forces.
  TJ163.23.W49 2007
  531'.6--dc22
                                        2006008858

Printed in the USA

CG/CG

Rourke Publishing

www.rourkepublishing.com – sales@rourkepublishing.com
Post Office Box 3328, Vero Beach, FL 32964

Table of Contents

Energy at the Construction Site	4
Using Energy	6
Energy from Gasoline	8
Energy from Batteries	10
Moving Energy	12
Energy from Electricity	14
Heat Energy	16
People Energy	18
Energy Safety	20
Try It!	22
Glossary	23
Index	24

Energy at the Construction Site

This is a **construction site**. People and **machines** work here. They need energy to work.

What kinds of energy do they need? Where does it come from? This book tells you about energy at a construction site.

Using Energy

Energy is the power to do work. Energy moves machines and people.

6

When workers use machines or **tools**, they are using energy. They use energy to move their bodies, too.

Energy from Gasoline

Workers pumped **gas** into this truck. The truck uses gas to run.

Gas does not make energy until the truck is on. Gas is **stored energy**.

Energy from Batteries

This drill uses batteries to run. Batteries are stored energy, too.

Batteries come in different sizes. Some have a lot of energy. Some have just a little.

Moving Energy

A wrecking ball swings into the building and breaks it down. It uses moving energy to work.

A hammer uses moving energy, too. The energy pushes the nail into the wood.

Energy from Electricity

A drill uses electricity to work. It gets to the drill from the cord.

This is a generator. It makes electricity at a construction site.

Heat Energy

This worker is using heat energy. He is **welding** metal. Welding melts pieces of metal together.

Welding uses heat energy. Some welding also makes light energy. Arc welding makes a bright light.

People Energy

Workers use energy all the time. They use energy in their bodies to walk, work, and talk.

People get energy from food. Our bodies turn the food into energy.

Energy Safety

Energy is useful at a construction site. But it can also be dangerous. Workers can trip on these cords.

Signs tell people about strong energy. Other signs tell workers about energy safety.

Try It!

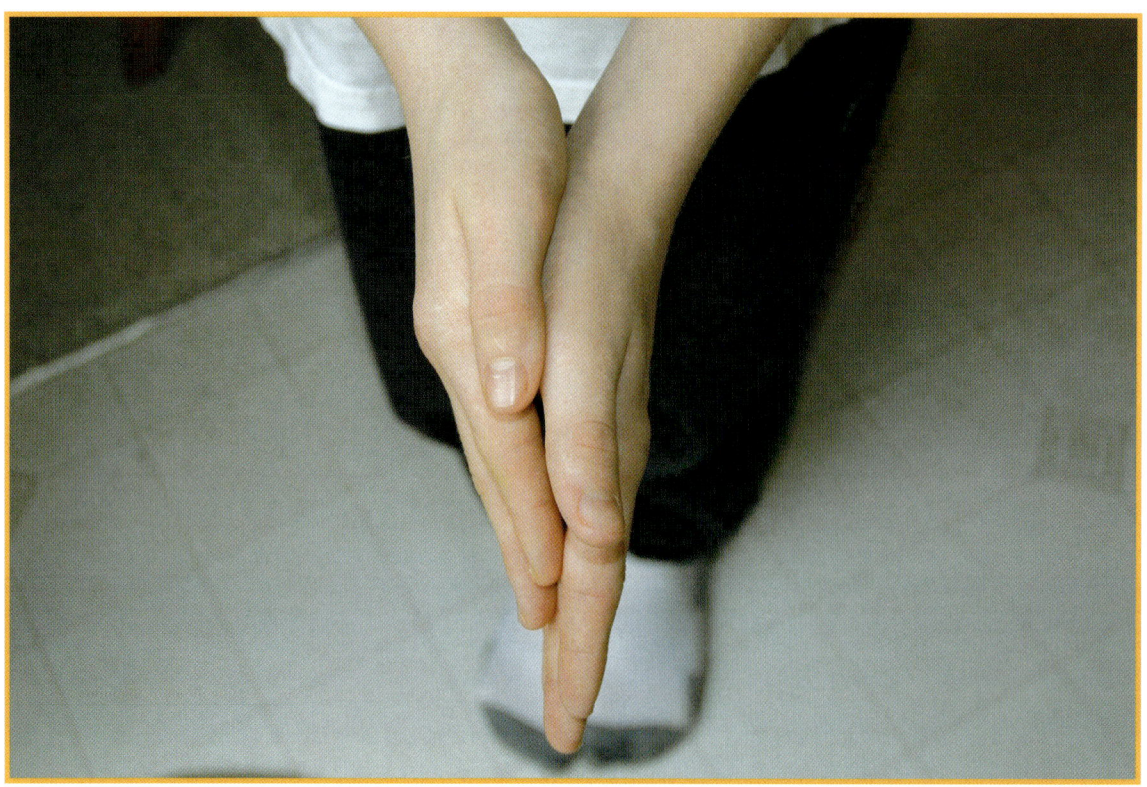

You can change your body's energy into heat energy. Rub your hands together quickly. Do you feel the heat?

GLOSSARY

construction site (kuhn STRUHKT shun SITE): a place where workers build

gas (GASS): fuel for cars and trucks, often called *gasoline*

machine (muh SHEEN): something that uses energy to help people work

stored energy (STORD EN ur jee): energy that can be used at a later time

tool (TOOL): something used to do work

welding (WELD ing): a way to put two pieces of metal together by melting them

INDEX

drill   10, 14
food   19
generator   15
light   17
truck   8, 9
work   4, 6, 12, 14, 18

FURTHER READING

Bowden, Rob. *Energy*. Kidhaven Press, 2004.
Bradley, Kimberly. *Energy Makes Things Happen.* HarperTrophy, New York: 2003.
Kilby, Don. *At a Construction Site.* Kids Can Press, 2003.

WEBSITES TO VISIT

http://www.eia.doe.gov/kids/:
http://iec.electricuniverse.com/flash/eu/education/louie/index.html
http://science.howstuffworks.com/engineering-channel.htm

ABOUT THE AUTHOR

Patty Whitehouse has been a teacher for 17 years. She is currently a Lead Science teacher in Chicago, where she lives with her husband and two teenage children. She is the author of more than 100 books about science for children.